The Story as Told

by
JALIL MAHMOUDI

ILLUSTRATIONS &
CALLIGRAPHY
by
RUSSELL ROBERTS

KALIMÁT PRESS
Los Angeles

For
Badri, Homa, Massood, Hoda,
Jason, and Naysan

Copyright © 1973, 1979
by Dr. Jalil Mahmoudi
Illustrations Copyright © 1979
by Russell Roberts
All Rights Reserved

Revised Edition

Library of Congress Catalog Card Number: 79-65925
ISBN 0-933770-10-3

Manufactured in the United States of America
80 81 82 83 10 9 8 7 6 5 6 4 3 2

The Story as Told

"I AM THAT I AM."
The Creator.
The Originator.
A hidden Treasure, Who loved to be known. He created His creatures to know Him.
He said, "Be,"
and it was.

He created your spirit
and called it

Adam.

He created your soul
and called it Eve.

He brought you from the
realm of absolute good
to the realm of choice between
Good and Not Good, called
the Tree of Good and Evil. He
gave you free will, and He
gave you His guidance

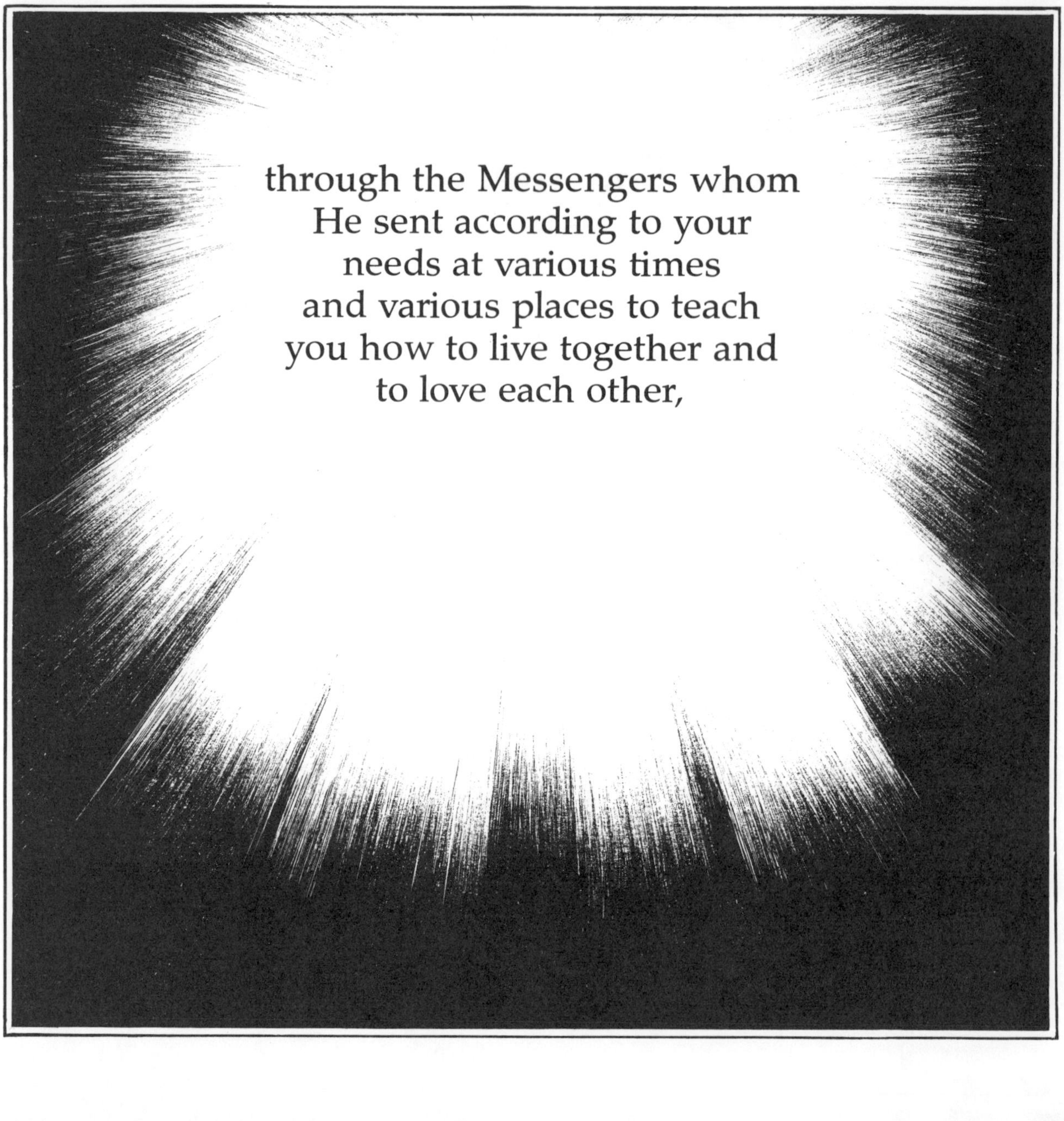

through the Messengers whom
He sent according to your
needs at various times
and various places to teach
you how to live together and
to love each other,

to teach you how to
achieve happiness in your lives
and order in your society,
so that you might live in
tranquillity and worship Him
with joy and serenity.

Through 𝔑oah, He summoned man "to the heaven of security and peace." He commissioned him to build the Ark—

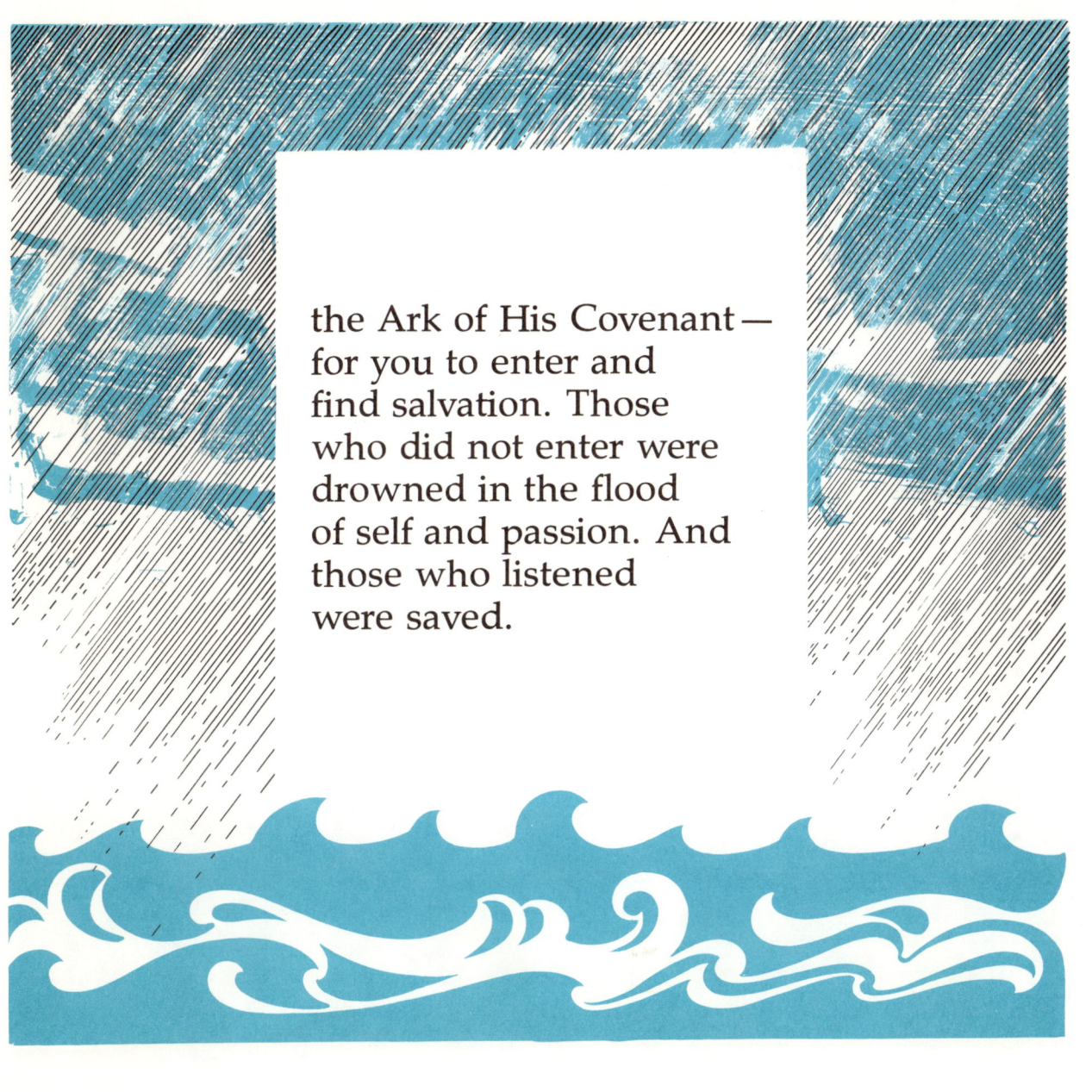

the Ark of His Covenant—
for you to enter and
find salvation. Those
who did not enter were
drowned in the flood
of self and passion. And
those who listened
were saved.

Then He sent Abraham, in Mesopotamia, to invite you to the court of His Oneness and to the light of righteousness. Some of you denounced this Friend of God

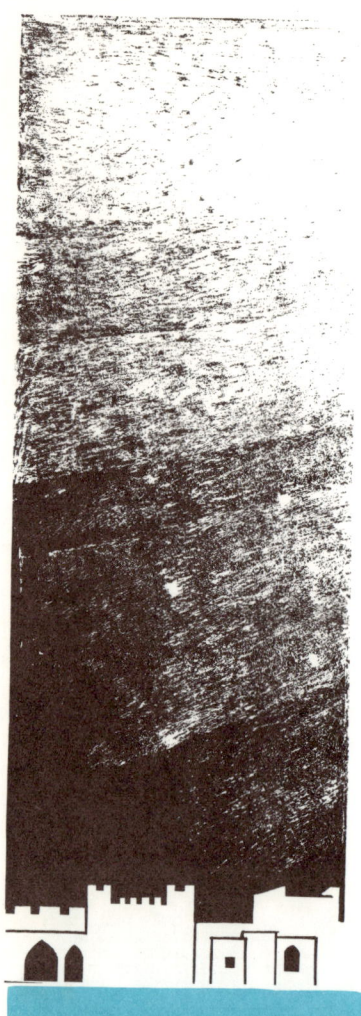

and kindled the fires of envy and rebellion. These fires were made to cool. You banished him to Syria; and that land became holy. You took away his rights; but his posterity was blessed.

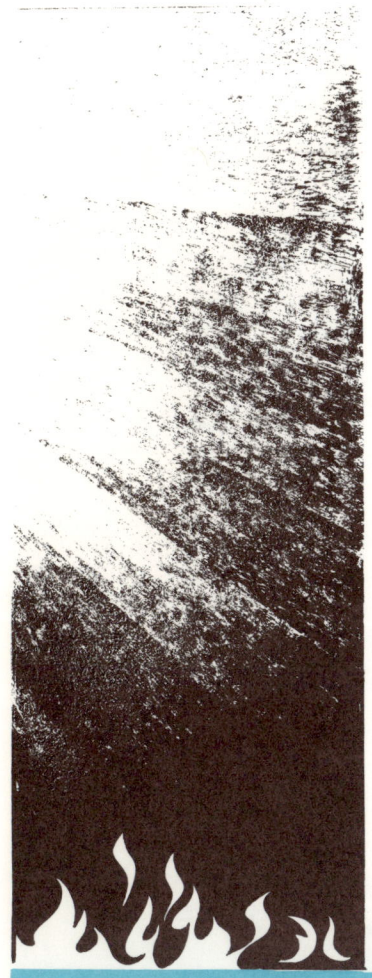

And He said
to Abraham,
"I will bless thee,
and make thy
name great;...
I will bless them
that bless thee,
and curse him
that curseth thee."

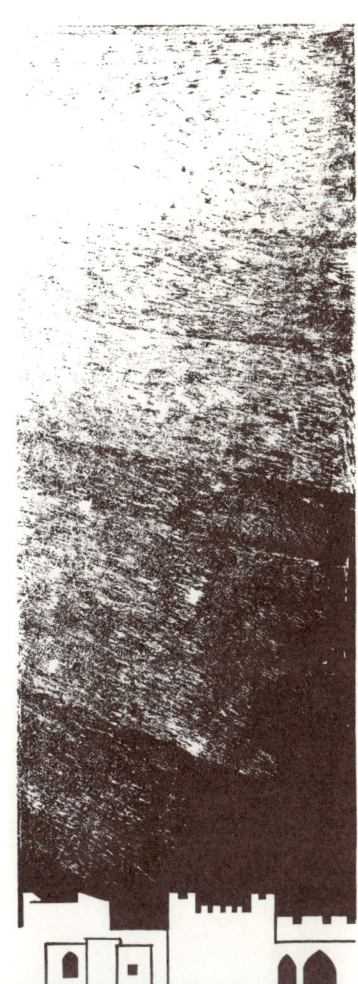

As a result of this Mission, multitudes entered under the protection of the shadow of His Oneness.

He gave
words
inscribed in the
Bhagavad Gita
and
the Vedas

to lead you to
His Oneness,
omnipresent and
supreme, to teach
you harmony, and
to prepare you to live
here and hereafter.
He told you that
your worldly

desires are doomed to frustration. This world is an illusion — Maya — a dream. There is a law — Karma — the force generated by your deeds.

It brings
rewards and punishments—
rebirth in the highest or
in the lowest forms of spiritual
being. Some of you understood
literally and materially, others
symbolically and spiritually.

And He taught you to pray: "O Knower of Births, bear us over every difficult crossing, yea, over all stumblings into evil as in a ship that travels over the waters. I meditate on thee

with a heart that
does the work
and I, mortal,
call to the Immortal.
O Will, O Knower
of Births, confirm
victory in us. By
the children of
my works may I
enjoy immortality."

Inscribed
in the Tripitaka,
the Three Baskets, are
Noble Truths and the way

to the
cessation of suffering.
Through the Middle Path,
the Noble Eightfold Path,

one should overcome anger with love, evil with good, greed with liberality, and lies with truth to attain the highest stage of happiness, selflessness, nothingness — Nirvana.

Meanwhile, He reaffirmed:
"Hurt not others in
ways that you yourself
would find hurtful."

And praise of all
the Buddhas:

"All Buddhas are glorious. There is not their equal upon the earth. They reveal to us the path of life. And we hail their appearance with pious reverence.

All the Buddhas teach the same truth. They point out the path to those who go astray. The truth is our hope and comfort. We gratefully accept its illimitable light."

In Egypt, through

oses,

His mouthpiece,

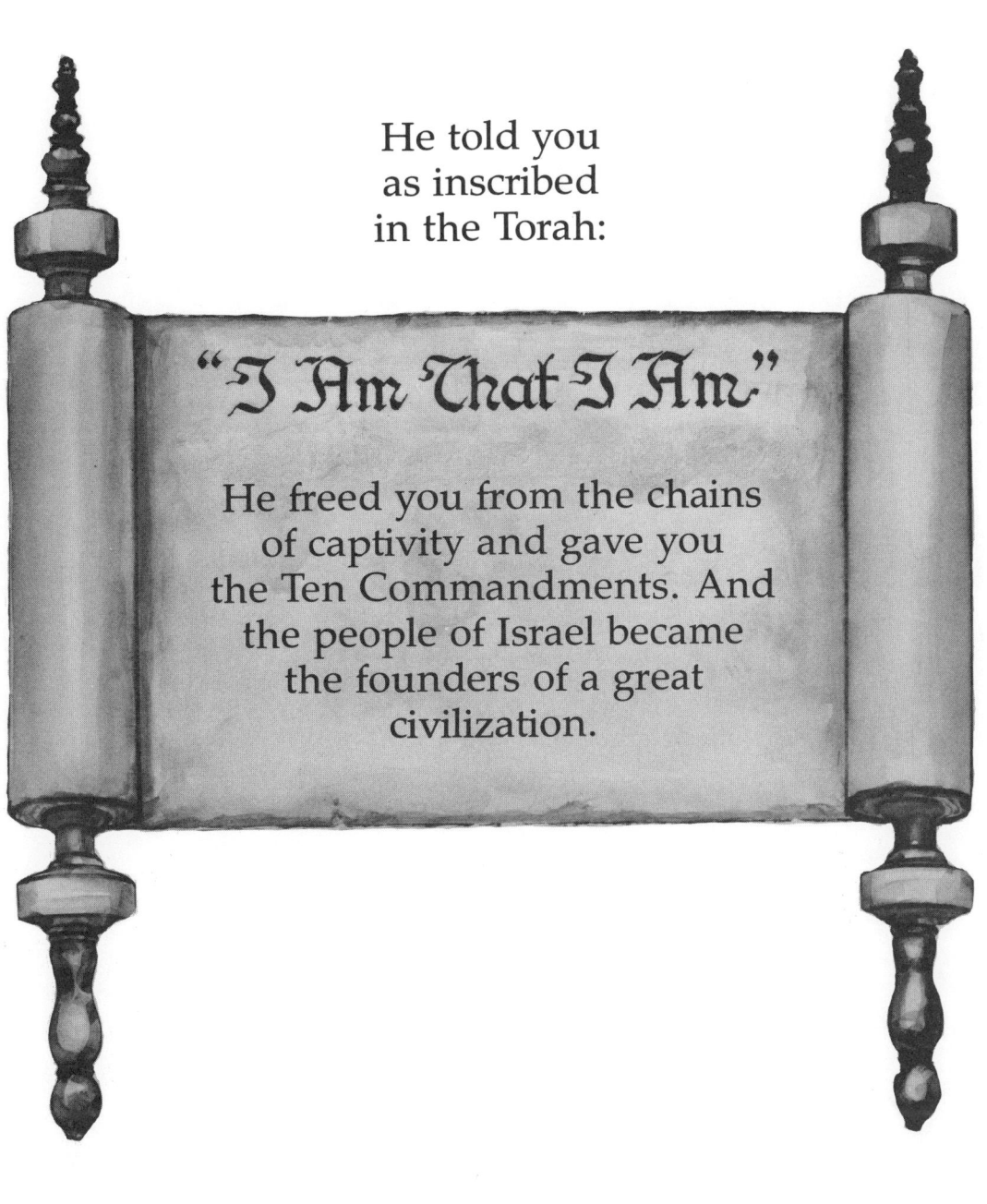

He told you as inscribed in the Torah:

"I Am That I Am"

He freed you from the chains of captivity and gave you the Ten Commandments. And the people of Israel became the founders of a great civilization.

He told you

that you are created in His image. He gave you the doctrine of Mitzvah and told you to obey His commandments.

"Love thy neighbor as thyself"

He promised you a Messianic Age when

all the nations "shall
beat their swords
into plowshares."

He reaffirmed:

> **What is hateful to you, do not to your fellowmen.**

That is the entire law.
All the rest
is commentary.

And Shema Yisrael: Hear, O Israel, the Lord is our God, the Lord is One. Blessed be His Name and His glorious kingdom forever and ever. Thou shalt love the Lord thy God with all thy heart, and with all thy soul, and with all thy might. And these words which I command thee this day shall be upon thy heart.

Thou shalt teach them diligently to thy children, speaking of them when thou sittest in thy house and when thou walkest by the way, when thou liest down and when thou risest up. Thou shalt bind them for a sign on thy hand, and they shall be as frontlets between thine eyes. And thou shalt write them upon the doorposts of thy house and upon thy gates.

In Persia,
through the Prophet
oroaster,

He gave you His words
in the Zend Avesta.
He told you,

"I am Ahura Mazda,
the God of Good.
Evil is Ahriman,
who is My enemy
as well as yours.
Help me by your good
thoughts, good works,
good deeds, and by
your cleanliness
to defeat Ahriman.

He further said:
"That nature alone
is good which
refrains from doing
unto another
whatsoever
is not good itself."
And He taught
you to pray:

Thou art Divine, I know O Lord Supreme. Thou wast the First, I know, when Life began. All thoughts and words and deeds of men shall bear the fruit as laid down in Thine Eternal Law — All good thoughts, all good works, all good deeds lead us on to 'Bahest,' the Beatitude of Paradise."

He
commissioned
His Spirit,

𝕴𝖊𝖘𝖚𝖘

in the Holy Land,

to give you the message of His love as inscribed in the Gospels. "Love your enemies. Bless them that curse you. Do good to them that hate you. Be ye therefore perfect, even as your Father which is in heaven is perfect."

These words were sent to regenerate your spirit, and to bring the glad tidings of peace on earth, good will toward men. Like the ones before him, and the ones after him, his spirit came not to destroy, but to fulfill.

He gave
his life
for your redemption
and salvation, and founded
a great
civilization.

Through him was also repeated: "All things whatsoever ye would that men should do to you, do ye even so to them: for this is the law and the prophets."
And a prayer.

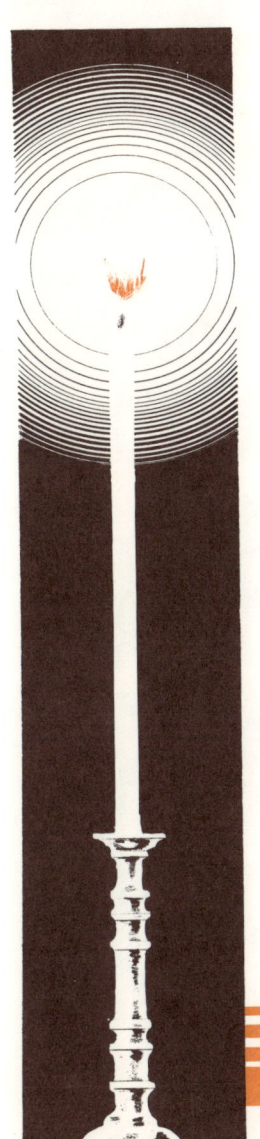
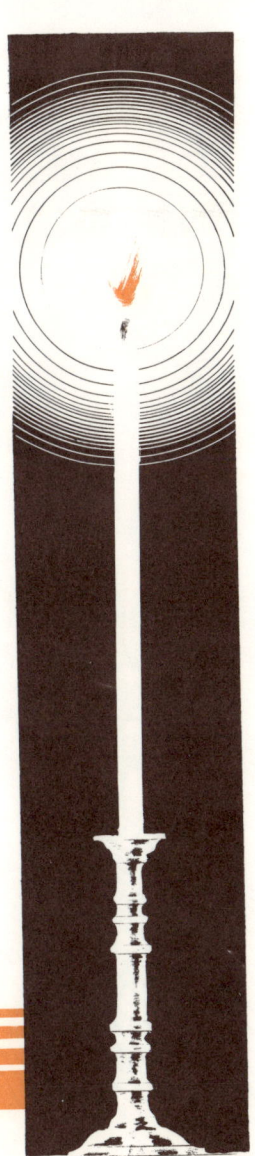

Our Father

which art in heaven,
Hallowed be thy name.
Thy kingdom come. Thy will be done
in earth, as it is in heaven. Give
us this day our daily bread. And
forgive us our debts, as we forgive
our debtors. And lead us not into
temptation, but deliver us from
evil: For thine is the kingdom, and
the power, and the glory, forever.

Amen

where the nomads knew only idolatry and plunder, He gave the Mission to bring them out of ignorance and lead them to His Path; to tell them of the One God, and of the former Messengers: Abraham, Zoroaster, Moses, Jesus, and others; and to teach them the divine laws.

Though illiterate, he was
given eloquent words
in His book, the Qur'án.
Though uneducated, he
became the greatest
educator. Through him,
Divine Knowledge was
renewed. From this came
his great civilization
the light of which shone

brightly against the darkness of ignorance and superstition, and shed its rays on many a land. And once more He confirmed: "No one of you is a believer until he desires for his brother that which he desires for himself."

And in the Qur'án: In the Name of God, the Compassionate, the Merciful.

Praise be to God, Lord of all the worlds!

The compassionate, the merciful!
King of the day of reckoning!
Thee only do we worship,
and to Thee do we cry for help.
Guide Thou us on the straight path,
the path of those to whom Thou hast
been gracious; with whom Thou art
not angry, and who go not astray.

to enlighten multitudes and prepare them for a greater Manifestation soon to appear. Through him, again, were confirmed all the Messengers of the past, and the glad tidings of the Promised One given.

He offered his life in this path to guide you to the Sun of Reality. He further told you that your guiding motive must be pure love, without fear of punishment or hope of reward:

"If you worship from fear, that is unworthy of the threshold of the holiness of God.... So also, if your gaze is on Paradise, and if you worship in hope of that; for then you have made God's creation a Partner with Him."

"Say: God sufficeth all things above all things, and nothing in the heavens or in the earth but God sufficeth. Verily, He is in Himself the Knower, the Sustainer, the Omnipotent."

to revive and regenerate the spiritual truths of faith and hope. And once more He repeated the Golden Rule: "Lay not on any soul a load which ye would not wish to be laid upon you, and desire not for any one the things ye would not desire for yourselves."

And prayer:
"O my God! O my God!
Unite the hearts of Thy servants
and reveal to them Thy great purpose.
May they follow Thy commandments and
abide in Thy law. Help them, O God, in their
endeavor, and grant them strength to serve
Thee. O God! leave them not to themselves,
but guide their steps by the light of knowledge,
and cheer their hearts by Thy love. Verily,
thou art their Helper and their Lord."

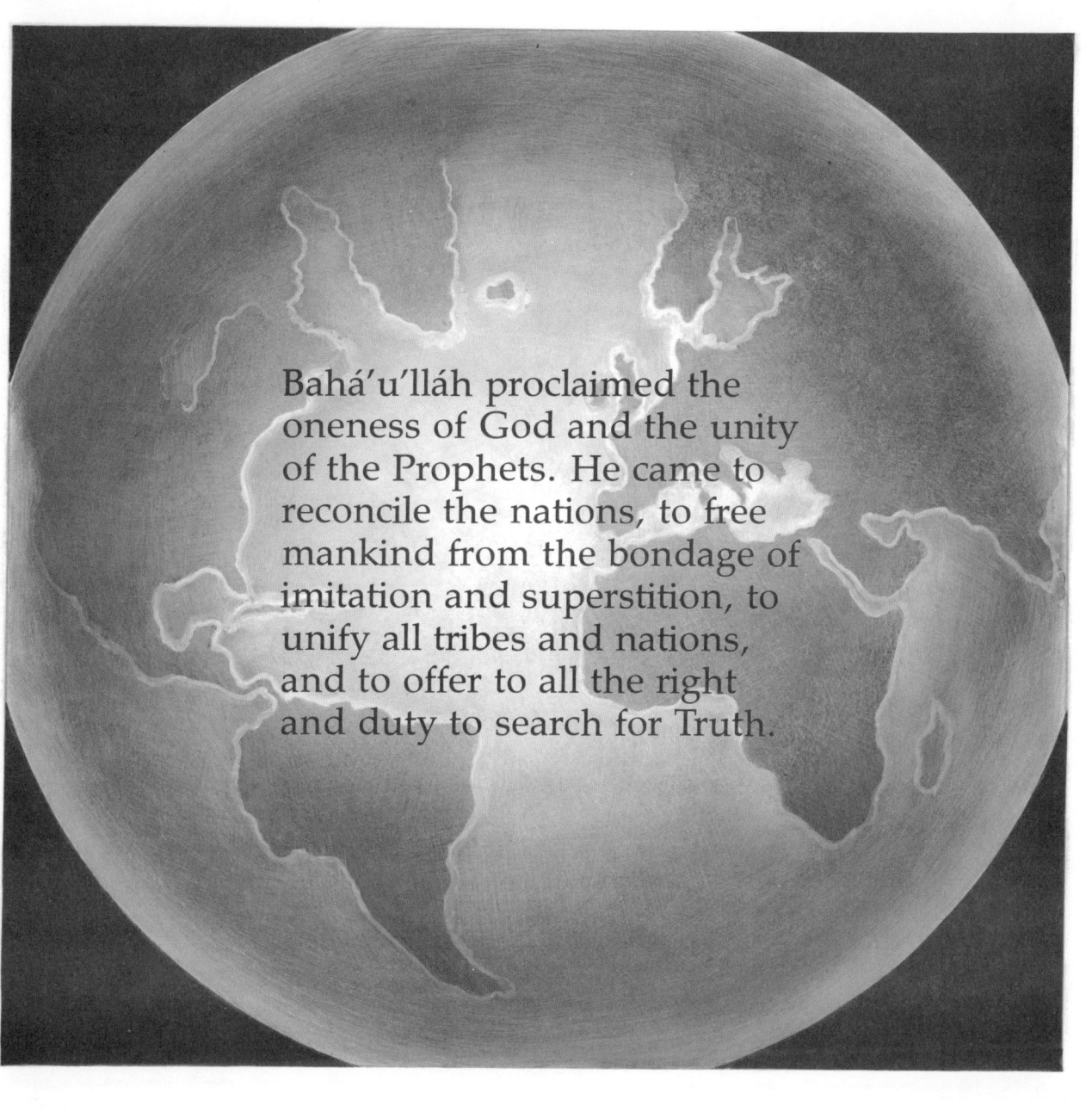

Bahá'u'lláh proclaimed the oneness of God and the unity of the Prophets. He came to reconcile the nations, to free mankind from the bondage of imitation and superstition, to unify all tribes and nations, and to offer to all the right and duty to search for Truth.

He gave
you the maturity to
live by laws which are
now proclaimed throughout
the world. He came to confirm
the Messengers of the past,
to fulfill their words,
to complete their
teachings,

and to
bring Universal
Peace under "one fold and
one shepherd." In this way,
one united world may be established
through love and justice,
in peace and harmony,
God's Kingdom
on earth.

Now that you have read *The Story as Told*, will you join me in this prayer:

"O Kind Lord! Thou Who art generous and merciful! We are the servants of Thy threshold and we are under the protection of Thy mercy.... Open the doors of Thy knowledge; let the light of faith shine. Unite and bring mankind into one shelter beneath the banner of Thy protection, so that they may become as waves of one sea, as leaves and branches of one tree, and may assemble beneath the shadow of the same tent. May they drink from the same fountain. May they be refreshed by the same breezes. May they obtain illumination from the same source of light and life. Thou art the Giver, the Merciful!"

–'Abdu'l-Bahá